a gift for

_____

from:

_____

Inspired by the 1950s landmark photographic exhibition, *"The Family of Man,"* M.I.L.K. began as an epic global search to develop a collection of extraordinary and geographically diverse images portraying humanity's Moments of Intimacy, Laughter and Kinship (M.I.L.K.). This search took the form of a photographic competition – probably the biggest, and almost certainly the most ambitious of its kind ever to be conducted. With a world-record prize pool, and renowned Magnum photographer Elliott Erwitt as Chief Judge, the M.I.L.K. competition attracted 17,000 photographers from 164 countries. Three hundred winning images were chosen from the over 40,000 photographs submitted to form the basis of the M.I.L.K. Collection.

The winning photographs were first published as three books titled *Family*, *Friendship* and *Love* in early 2001, and are now featured in a range of products worldwide, in nine languages in more than 20 countries. The M.I.L.K. Collection also forms the basis of an international travelling exhibition.

The M.I.L.K. Collection portrays unforgettable images of human life, from its first fragile moments to its last. They tell us that the rich bond that exists between families and friends is universal. Representing many diverse cultures, the compelling and powerful photographs convey feelings experienced by people around the globe. Transcending borders, the M.I.L.K. imagery reaches across continents to celebrate and reveal the heart of humanity.

www.milkphotos.com

MOTHERS

with love

M·I·L·K

MOMENTS INTIMACY LAUGHTER KINSHIP

Before you were conceived I wanted you.
Before you were born I loved you.
Before you were here an hour I would die for you.
This is the miracle of life.

[MAUREEN HAWKINS]

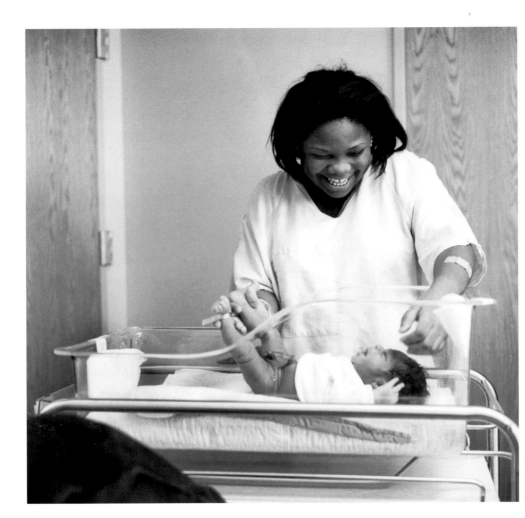

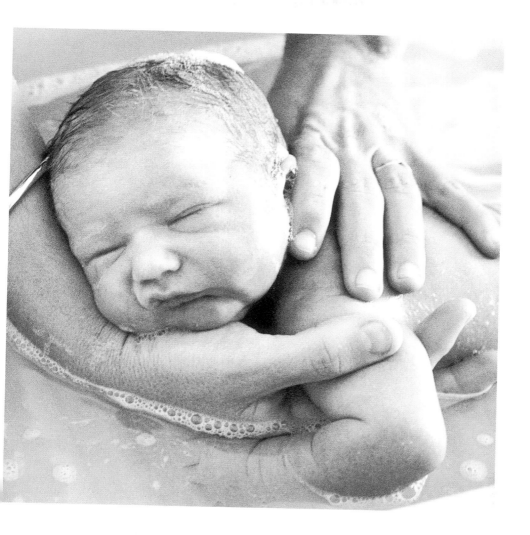

Oh what a power is motherhood.

[EURIPIDES]

So many scars, my arms, my back. I thought
I would never marry,
no-one would love me.

But I was so wrong.
This picture of me, and my Thomas,
my angel – it's a picture of love.

[KIM PHUC]

I do not love him because he is good,
but because he is my... child.

[RABINDRANATH TAGORE]

You cannot catch
a child's spirit
by running after it.
You must stand still and for love
it will soon itself return.

[ARTHUR MILLER]

So sweet and precious is family life.

Joy is not in things, it is in us.

We find a delight in the
beauty and happiness
of children that makes the heart
too big for the body.

[RALPH WALDO EMERSON]

There is no greater miracle
than watching a child being **born.**

[JAMES MCBRIDE]

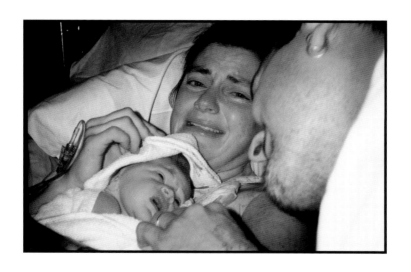

Hold tenderly that
which you cherish.

What do you think about
when you think about love?
Mother's love,
the love of children –
which is so beautiful,
so strong, so joyful,

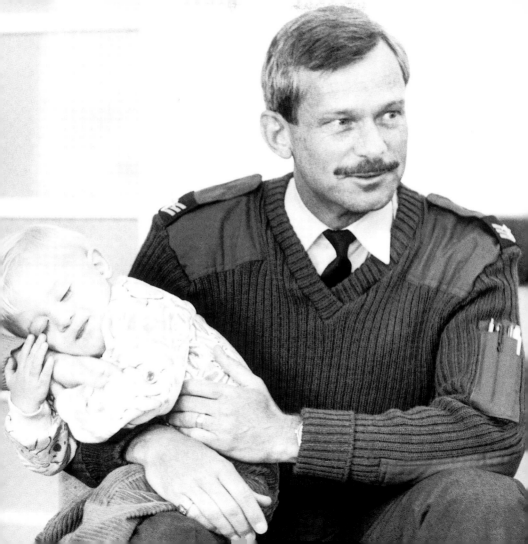

The best and most **beautiful** things in the world cannot be seen or even touched. They must be felt with the heart.

Pages 6–7
© Linda Sole, UK
When her daughter Judith became pregnant, English photographer Linda Sole decided to make this her next project. Judith is enjoying a bath on a hot summer day in Woolwich, London – two months later a daughter, Rose, was born.

Page 9
© Gerald Botha, South Africa
Good morning in Durban, South Africa – the photographer's wife, Aileen, greets their three-month-old son, Eden.

Page 10
© Mark LaRocca, USA
A mother's joyous smile as she admires her newborn baby, Cedric, born 36 hours ago at this hospital in Newton, Massachusetts, USA.

Page 11
© Kelvin Patrick Jubb, Australia
Fewer than 24 hours have elapsed since this baby was born. In a busy hospital ward in Penrith, Australia, the baby is cradled by his mother as he experiences his first bath.

Page 12 and front cover
© Milo Stewart Jr, USA
In Cooperstown, New York, new mother Leslie is enchanted with her baby son Bartow.

Pages 14–15
© Yew Fatt Siew, Malaysia
A Buddhist festival at Labuleng Lamasery in Gansu, China – in sub-zero temperatures, a Tibetan mother's embrace offers protection and warmth.

Pages 16–17
© Anne Bayin, Canada
Kim grew up thinking boys would find her unattractive because of her scars, but today she is married and living in Canada. She is a Goodwill Ambassador for UNESCO. This photograph celebrates the first birthday of Kim's son, Thomas.

Kim Phuc was the subject of the most famous picture of the Vietnam War. Taken in 1972, the photograph showed Kim – "the girl in the picture" – badly burned by napalm.

Page 19
© Venkata Sunder Rao Pampana (Sunder), India
A tender touch – a young girl looks after her baby sister asleep in a hammock made from her mother's sari. Without a permanent home, the family lives on the streets of Vijayawada in India.

Page 20
© Thomas Patrick Kiernan, Ireland
A young boy shares his delight with his mother as he paddles in the water on Coney Island, New York.

Page 21
© Jia Lin Wu, China
Mother and son in Butuo County, Sichuan province, China.

Pages 22–23
© Stacey P Morgan, USA
In New York, Anne and her young son Robert discover that the bedroom is the perfect place for hide and seek.

Pages 24–25
© Juan P Barragán, Ecuador
Keeping tradition alive near Lake San Pablo, Ecuador. Four generations of an Imbabura Indian family prepare their hair in the time-honored way – from right to left: Mama-Rosa, Rosa, Rosa Elena and Miriam.

Page 26
© Neil Selkirk, USA
Open wide – on a trip to the beach in Wellfleet, Massachusetts, USA, nothing interests Zane more than her mother, Susan.

Pages 28–29
© Binode Kumar Das, India
After a hard day's work in West Bengal, India, a mother is delighted to return to the company of her children.

Pages 30–31
© Russell Shakespeare, Australia
In Manly, New South Wales, Australia, five-month-old Camille has a captive audience in her mother, Toni, and visiting grandparents, Margaret and Handley.

Page 33
© Álvaro Diaz, Brazil
10-month-old Gabriel and his mother, Paula. The photographer captured this picture of his son in Florianopolis, Brazil.

Page 34
© Auke Vleer, The Netherlands
Young cousins – Pol, Joris, Dorus and Rik – enjoy being taken for a ride on the beach in Baratier, France.

Page 35
© Natassa Tselepoglou, Greece
Family life in Halkidiki, Greece. Three-year-old Lia and her mother, Daphne, put their feet up and share a fairy tale.

Page 36
© Linda Heim, USA
Lynn and her 10-month-old son, Casey, try a new variation of rock-a-bye-baby on the shore of Burden Lake in New York state, USA.

Pages 38–39
© Auke Vleer, The Netherlands
Five-year-old Pol with his aunt, Letty, on a family vacation in Baratier, France. While grandmother Fanny admires the view of the lake, their dog prefers to take a nap.

Pages 40–41 and back cover
© Stefano Azario, UK
Like mother, like daughter – at a New York airport, there's still time for nine-month-old Verity and her mother, Lydzia, to play before the long flight home to England.

Page 43
© Barbara Judith Exeter, New Zealand,
A mother's face is a picture of relief after the birth of her first child in Hastings, New Zealand. After 32 hours in labor, Linda is exhausted, but ecstatic, as father Wayne admires baby Braeden, only five minutes old.

Pages 44–45
© Kamthorn Pongsutiyakorn, Thailand
A grandmother with her grand-daughter in the backyard of their home in Chonburi, Thailand.

Page 46
© Fredé Spencer, Denmark
Water baby – swimming under water comes perfectly naturally to baby Louis. He and his mother, Dimiti, enjoy a swimming class for "Little Dippers" in London, England.

Page 48
© Lloyd Erlick, Canada
Family portrait in Toronto, Canada – proud mother Caitlin gently holds six-month-old Shai as she reaches out to greet her great-grandmother, Natalie.

Page 49
© Jarek Kret, Poland
In a remote village on the west coast of Madagascar, a young woman is oblivious to the photographer's presence as he captures this tender image of her watching over her young child.

Pages 50–51
© Abel Naim, Venezuela
During a workshop for the underprivileged communities of Caracas, Venezuela, children learn how to communicate with others and to express their emotions. As the instructor, Durbin, gives her young student a hug, their faces light up with love and happiness.

Page 53
© Tomas D W Friedmann, Italy
Protected and loved – in the Masailand of Tanzania, a Masai mother gently carries her young child.

Pages 54–55
© Edmond Terakopian, UK
British Royal Air Force sergeant John has just returned from the Gulf War to his wife, Sharon, and their two-year-old son, Phillip. Their reunion was captured during a press conference in Stanmore, Middlesex, England.

Page 56–57
© Lynn Goldsmith, USA
A little girl holds tightly to her grandmother's hand as they walk together in Arles, France.

Page 59
© Frank White, USA
In Houston, Texas, USA, Jo-Anne cuddles her five-year-old daughter, Ellen, in a loving embrace. They are smiling at the photographer – husband and father Frank White.

© 2004 PQ Publishers Limited. Published under license from M.I.L.K. Licensing Limited.

All copyrights of the photographic images are owned by the individual photographers who have granted M.I.L.K. Licensing Limited the right to use them.

First published by Helen Exley Giftbooks in 2003,
16 Chalk Hill, Watford, Herts, WD19 4BG, UK.

First published by Helen Exley Giftbooks LLC in 2004,
185 Main Street, Spencer, MA 01562, USA.

4 6 8 10 12 11 9 7 5

ISBN 1 86187 604 1

Concept designed by Kylie Nicholls. This edition designed by Holly Stevens. Printed in China.
Back cover quotation by James McBride.

M • I • L • K™
MOMENTS INTIMACY LAUGHTER KINSHIP